T0198745

BEHOLD THE TREE

NATHALIA EQUIHUA
ILLUSTRATED BY MARCELLA GIBSON

This book is a work of non-fiction. Unless otherwise noted, the author and the publisher make no explicit guarantees as to the accuracy of the information contained in this book and in some cases, names of people and places have been altered to protect their privacy.

WestBow Press books may be ordered through booksellers or by contacting:

WestBow Press
A Division of Thomas Nelson & Zondervan
1663 Liberty Drive
Bloomington, IN 47403
www.westbowpress.com
1 (866) 928-1240

Interior Image Credit: Marcella Gibson

Scripture taken from the New King James Version®. Copyright © 1982 by Thomas Nelson. Used by permission. All rights reserved.

ISBN: 978-1-9736-8412-1 (sc)
ISBN: 978-1-9736-8413-8 (e)

Library of Congress Control Number: 2020901209

Print information available on the last page.

WestBow Press rev. date: 01/27/2020

WESTBOW
PRESS®
A DIVISION OF THOMAS NELSON
& ZONDERVAN

How often have we heard God created the universe, we are all one, and we are all connected? I'm a believer! While meditating and praying about a challenge in my life, our Lord began to speak to me about the trees before me. I have written His spoken words in this book so that all will understand that our changes are in sync with all the earthly changes orchestrated by God. Hopefully these words will be read again and again whenever there is a change in the reader's life. Trees are very special to me (I've even hugged a few) so it is no wonder that God has given the tree as an example of how to be still, stay deeply rooted in Him, have faith, and soon your life will be bursting with newness.

Read BEHOLD THE TREE and you will be able to ride the tidal waves of change because you know your summer is near.

Gen. 2:9 And out of the ground the Lord God made every tree grow that is pleasant to the sight and good for food. The tree of life was also in the midst of the garden, and the tree of knowledge of good and evil.

I cried out, "My Lord my God, I want so much to be Your love in flesh for all of those that you send to me. There seems to be an endless need for healing, comforting, and finances. Even though my ministry is only a tiny fraction of others, I understand why Jesus constantly went away and prayed to you, Heavenly Father. Galatians 6:9 says, "So let us not grow weary of doing what is good for in due season we shall reap. Do not loose heart." But my energy level seems so low. I feel drained! Father, just how far am I to extend myself to others?

Matt. 14:23 And when He had sent the multitude away, He went up on the mountain by himself to pray.

And the Lord answered, "Behold the tree My child! The branches stretch so tall that they appear to touch the sky, but they do not. Some are as wide as they are tall. This is how you are to reach out to others. But behold, there is an end! They do not go on indefinitely and where these branches end, another tree is nearby extending its branches.

So it is with life. All are My children and I tend to their needs as they come to Me. What is not received through you, will be received through another vessel. There are many vessels. It is for you to pray and listen as you minister to others. Listen and I will tell you when to let go of the person and their needs, trusting that I will continue to care for them through another. Pray, listen, and have faith."

2 Cor. 8:13-15 For I do not mean that others should be eased and you burdened; but in equality, that now at this time your abundance may supply their lack, that their abundance also may supply your lack that there may be equality. As it is written, He who gathered much had nothing left over, and he who gathered little had no lack.

PS. 32:8 I will instruct you and teach you in the way you should go.

1Cor. 12:4,5,11 There are diversities of gifts, but the same spirit. There are diversities of ministries, but the same Lord. But one and the same Spirit works all these distributing to each one individually as He wills.

I am amazed at how most tree branches grow toward the Heavenly light above. And when they are fully grown, no matter how big or small, they are forever lifted in praise of their creator. Their roots, which are as long as the branches we see, are deeply buried in the soil.

Oh Lord, help me to be as firmly rooted in You as the mightiest tree is rooted into the earth.

Heavenly Father please also give me the strength I need to lift my arms like the branches of those mighty trees in continuous praise of You.

Col. 2:6-7 As you therefore have received Christ Jesus the Lord, so walk in Him rooted and built up in Him and established in faith; as you have been taught, abounding in it with thanksgiving.

However, all trees do not lift their branches. There is an exception, the Weeping Willow Tree and others in its family. Their branches do not reach up in praise of its creator. And yet it displays such strength and beauty. Behold the Willow Tree! Its roots are deeper than most. And its lovely branches bow in humble adoration of our Lord!

Heavenly Father I pray for the grace to look deeper and not make hasty judgments. What majestic beauty there is in this tribute to God. Dare I even dream to remain so humble for a lifetime?

1 Peter 5:5-6 God resist the proud but gives grace to the humble. Therefore, humble yourself under the mighty hand of God that He may exalt you.

My child Behold the tree! It is green and obviously full of life. Gentle and strong winds blow the branches of leaves. And yet they cling on and life continues to flow through them. It is summer and the leaves are green and strong. We have summer seasons also; everything flows comfortably, peacefully, and orderly. Challenges come but do not disturb our peace and harmony.

2 Cor. 4:8-10 We are hard pressed on every side, yet not crushed, we are perplexed, but not in despair; persecuted, but not forsaken; struck down, but not destroyed always carrying about in the body the dying of the Lord Jesus, that the life of Jesus may be manifested in our body.

Fall comes and the leaves appear to lose their life. They change colors (red, yellow, orange, and brown) and fall from the branches.

We have fall seasons also. No, we do not change colors; but our habits, emotions, or inner spirit changes. These changes cause us to lose our peacefulness and disturb our comfort level with others and ourselves. Negative forces emerge such as anger, anxiety, fear, and unforgiveness. As we pray to our heavenly Father, these negative forces leave, and we are able to survive our fall/autumn season.

John 10:10 The thief does not come except to steal and to kill and destroy. I have come that they may have life abundantly.

Behold the winter tree! All the leaves have fallen and only the branches remain. There is no sign of life. It is completely bare. Even though life is not visible as in the vibrant green leaves of summer, life is there. The tree stands stripped of its richness, and yet its branches remain lifted to God and waits to be nourished and richly clothed again. It bares the freezing cold as it stands trusting that God will bring forth the rich green life again.

Heavenly Father grant me the grace to be still without worry or complaining, but rather in praise of You in the winter of my life. Father I pray for that calm assurance as the winter tree. Even though I may not see the process, grant me the grace to know You are healing me. You are sustaining me and bringing about a new richness of life within and around me.

Heb. 13:15 Therefore by Him let us continually offer the sacrifice of praise to God, that is, the fruit of our lips, giving thanks to His name.

Deut. 31:5 Have I not told you to be strong and of good courage.

PS. 46:10 Be still and know that I am God.

The season is spring and signs of life all around. All the seasonal trees are covered with tiny sprouts of green leaves. Some even have blossoms of beautiful fragrant flowers and many bear fruits.

Heavenly Father open my eyes to the signs of my new beginnings. Perhaps it's a healthier lifestyle and body, an increase in prosperity, or a new relationship. Help me Lord to see and give thanks to You for even the tiniest sign of Your loving presence.

2 Cor. 5:17 Therefore, if anyone is in Christ, he/she is a new creation; old things have passed away; Behold all things have become new.

Matt. 25:36 I was naked, and You clothed me.

Miraculously the tree is once again clothed with beautiful green leaves. Summer has returned. There are so many leaves the branches are barely visible. How can this be? Did not this tree stand bare for months? How does this happen again and again throughout the entire life of this tree? It happens because the tree never doubts. It knows that even though changes come in Autumn and there are winters when there is no visible sign of life, Spring and Summer are coming.

We also must believe deep within that weather we are experiencing summer, fall, winter or spring God is with us through every seasonal experience.

Matt.6:31-33 Therefore do not worry saying "What shall we eat? Or what shall we drink or what shall we wear? But seek first the kingdom of God and His righteousness and all these shall be added to you.

Heb. 13:5 I will never leave you nor forsake you.

Phil. 4:11 Not that I speak in regard to need, for I have learned in whatever state I am, to be content.

And then I asked the Lord, "What about the Evergreen Tree?" These trees never change. Therefore, the branches are never bare. Some branches stretch up in praise, some straight out as a sign of standing firm, and some bow in humble adoration. The leaves/needles remain green summer, fall, winter, and spring.

Few of us have reached the spiritual level of the Evergreen Trees. Few of us can say no to every temptation before us and remain steadfast in our commitment to God. Most of us experience the change to the fall/autumn season, which leads to the bareness of winter.

Heavenly Father could I possibly hope to be as the Evergreen Tree? How I long to have the peace that surpasses mankind and a complete attitude of gratitude. It is when we lack appreciation and fail to thank God for where we are in our life that we make bad decisions. Thus, the changes made bring about negative forces in our lives.

PS.1 Blessed is the man who walks not in the counsel of the ungodly nor stands in the path of sinners, nor sits in the seat of the scornful; but his delight is in the law of the Lord, and in His law he meditates day and night .He shall be like a tree planted by the rivers of water, that brings forth its fruit in its season, whose leaf also shall not wither, whatever he does shall prosper.

James 1:14 But each one is tempted when he is drawn away by his own desires and enticed.

From this time forth hopefully each tree you see will serve as a reminder to worship our Heavenly Father. The branches lifted are a reminder to praise Him wherever you are. Perhaps you are in a place where you can't lift your hands, but you can lift your heart anywhere. Or perhaps you may encounter a Willow tree with branches bowing in humble adoration. You may not want to bow down at the mall, but you can humble your heart anywhere and surrender your will to God. Or finally, perhaps you may see an Evergreen Tree with branches sticking straight out signaling stand firm. You can't stand firm if you're driving or crossing the street. But you can stand firm in your faith in God when negative forces are telling you to do otherwise.

There are many similarities between trees and humans. The Bible tells us "Let everything that has breath praise the Lord." Thank God for the trees that are all around to remind us to do just that. Amen!

PS.96:12 Let the field be joyful and all that is within it. Then all the trees of the woods will rejoice before the Lord.

Heb. 13:15 Therefore by Him let us continually offer the sacrifice of praise to God, that is, the fruit of our lips, giving thanks to Him.

Printed in the United States
By Bookmasters